OLD WORLD KITCHENS AND BATHROOMS

D1540927

OLD WORLD KITCHENS AND BATHROOMS
A Design Guide

TINA SKINNER & MELISSA CARDONA

Schiffer Publishing Ltd

4880 Lower Valley Road, Atglen, PA 19310 USA

Published by Schiffer Publishing Ltd.
4880 Lower Valley Road
Atglen, PA 19310
Phone: (610) 593-1777; Fax: (610) 593-2002
E-mail: Info@schifferbooks.com

For the largest selection of fine reference books on this
and related subjects, please visit our web site at
www.schifferbooks.com
We are always looking for people to write books on
new and related subjects. If you have an idea for a
book please contact us at the above address.

This book may be purchased from the publisher.
Include $3.95 for shipping.
Please try your bookstore first.
You may write for a free catalog.

In Europe, Schiffer books are distributed by
Bushwood Books
6 Marksbury Ave.
Kew Gardens
Surrey TW9 4JF England
Phone: 44 (0) 20 8392-8585;
Fax: 44 (0) 20 8392-9876
E-mail: info@bushwoodbooks.co.uk
Free postage in the U.K., Europe; air mail at cost.

Library of Congress Cataloging-in-Publication Data:

Skinner, Tina.
  Old world kitchens and bathrooms : a design and guide /
by Tina Skinner.
    p. cm.
  ISBN 0-7643-2078-5 (pbk.)
1. Kitchens—Pictorial works. 2. Bathrooms—Pictorial
works. 3. Interior decoration—Europe—Influence—Pictorial
works. I. Title.
NK2117.K5S67 2004
747.7'8—dc22
                                    2004005730

Designed by John P. Cheek
Type set in AlgerianBasD/Korinna BT

ISBN: 0-7643-2078-5
Printed in China

CONTENTS

INTRODUCTION

English Country, Tuscan Style, French Provencal...Phrases such as these have become hot buzz words for contemporary home design. Today's homeowners are searching for something from the past for their homes. Amidst appliances that can freeze food in seconds flat, ovens that cook with convection, and faucets that can be set to dispense water teakettle hot, there is a sense that something is missing. So today's top designers are helping to fill that void for discerning homeowners, providing the same standards of excellence for the framework around that high-tech gadgetry – the cabinetry and countertops, the stove surrounds and hoods. Moreover, they are providing a context of continuity, of enduring quality and ambiance. In constructing kitchens for today's world, the inspiration, the materials, and the craftsmanship are being resurrected from the old.

Fine woodworking skills are being employed for furniture-style cabinetry, and to recreate the hand-carved detailing of yesteryear. Manmade materials such as laminates and "solid surfaces" are being shelved in favor of earthy, enduring granites and other natural stones, as well as solid-wood butcher-block surfaces friendly to the knife.

The décor complements the timeless materials and craftsmanship, too. Stucco range hoods, brick walls, and flagstone flooring are popular options. And tile backsplashes and floors embody the same earthen qualities that homeowners have enjoyed for centuries. Wrought iron may characterize the fixtures and ornaments, or fine crystal lighting may add the luster of a bygone era. Faux finishing can be used to add the patina of age, or simply to create a mural that opens an imaginary view to the French countryside or an Italian vineyard.

By creating an environment rich in timeless materials, a homeowner gains a sense of permanence, even in a completely new home. The design may strike a chord with one's ethnic heritage, or simply reflect a desire for the finer things from the past.

So, with manufacturers bandying about words like "chateau" and "villa," with colors and finishes in "merlot," "cabernet," and "terracotta," the stage is set for a virtual Renaissance in European design sensibility.

KITCHENS

A stone mantle hood adds a rustic complement to the elegant styling of more ornate design elements in the kitchen – like the light fixture above the center island and the faux-finished barrel vaulted ceiling and walls. *Courtesy of Harrison Design Associates*

This grand and elegant kitchen promotes feelings of comfort and stability with gorgeous detailed carvings on the cabinetry, intricate shapes, and distressed finishes. The Continental European design theme encompasses the whole room—even the ceiling. Stucco was painted with decorative motifs and a faux finish to give it an aged look. This kitchen is nothing short of extraordinary and breathtakingly beautiful. *Courtesy of Wood-Mode*

Continued on following pages

The owners of the kitchen wanted the dining area to have an Italian Villa theme. The designers chose a rich burnished furniture finish with wrought iron accents, along with crystal ice glass inserts, clipped corners, carvings, and Louis Philippe drawerheads to create the theme. Exposed beams and the unfinished tile flooring all add to the space's sense of history. *Courtesy of Wood-Mode*

A kitchen suited for a royal family features marvelous window treatments and faux-finished walls. The effect is nothing less than regal. Finely carved cabinetry with marble countertops and backsplash would make any queen happy to reign over this kitchen. *Courtesy of Harrison Design Associates*

Walls tiled floor to ceiling, furniture-style cabinetry, and a carved limestone hood give this elegant kitchen an old European feel. Granite countertops edged with limestone and the coffered ceiling add formality. *Courtesy of Design Galleria, Ltd.*

Hexagonal tile flooring adds color and interest to a kitchen made for entertaining guests. Tile backsplashes and detailed carvings give this modern kitchen an old world twist. *Courtesy of Harrison Design Associates*

A rich black finish creates a bold stroke in this kitchen. Turned legs move cabinetry into the league of custom furnishings. *Courtesy of Wellborn Cabinet, Inc.*

Stained glass windows add color and interest to a kitchen dominated by white tile walls. A tall wooden cupboard showcases grandma's tea set, and tall chairs at the island counter are upholstered like the table chairs. A mosaic motif in front of the stove adds color, interest, and age to the floor. *Courtesy of Wood-Mode/Designer John A. Buscarello* (Continued on following pages)

This is a wonderful reproduction of former times, with today's conveniences. This kitchen starts with the great hearth, where one would have cooked years ago. Today, however, it is the perfect draw for center island seating. Wood beams and a window seat add charm and authenticity to the architecture, while a multi-tone paint scheme softens and ages the walls. Classic cabinetry mimics the wood craftsmanship of seasoned furnishings. *Courtesy of KraftMaid Cabinetry*

A molded metal ceiling adds old world flavor and contemporary flair to this kitchen. A reproduction wood burning stove hung with copper pots and faux finished walls make the space feel like grandma's old kitchen. *Courtesy of Wood-Mode/Designers Pamela Baird, CKD and Eddie Saunders*

Window treatments and upholstered chairs add color this kitchen. Exposed distressed wood beams provide a sense of comfort and age, while contemporary conveniences make cooking a grand pleasure. *Courtesy of Harrison Design Associates*

Two sides of a long wall are divided into distinct purposes in this spacious kitchen. On the one side, stainless steel countertop and closed cabinetry denotes the area's working nature, while glass-fronted cabinetry and a wood counter shine for display on the other side. *Courtesy of Plain & Fancy Custom Cabinetry*

A cottage kitchen exudes a rustic quality with its textured walls and unfinished mantle hood. The walls look like they were spackled in blue and white back when grandpa was just a boy, and the wooden plank table adds to that aged effect. *Courtesy of Wood-Mode*

Knotty pine cabinets with a natural finish compliment the adobe plastered walls and the reclaimed timber beams. The flooring was also made of reclaimed lumber, creating a warm and inviting atmosphere. A long countertop and row of cabinets provide plenty of preparation and storage space. *Courtesy of Aged Woods, Inc.*

Casual and charming characterizes this Provence-inspired kitchen. A French monk's table and a French dresser were teamed up with fitted cabinetry in three types of wood and two custom finishes to create a distinctly warm and intimate space. *Courtesy of Plain & Fancy Custom Cabinetry*

Old world gets a facelift with the addition of Asian and country elements. The result is a spectacular culinary concoction that will have you asking for seconds...and thirds. *Courtesy of Wood-Mode/Designer Jane Victor*

©Norman McGrath

29

Accessories – copper, candelabra, and goblets – add to the aura of ancient feasts and celebrations in this space. Camel glass window designs draw on Alpine tradition, as does the lace-like cutout pattern in the woodwork trim. *Courtesy of KraftMaid Cabinetry*

Opposite page:
A fruit motif is repeated in the window treatments, leaded glass windows, carved detailing on the cabinets, and wall hangings. Upholstered chairs complement the rug, and display shelves above a desk allow the owners of this kitchen to show off their favorite trinkets. *Courtesy of Harrison Design Associates*

An armchair at the desk harks back to earlier eras, as does the wrought iron craftsmanship in two barstools at the counter. *Courtesy of KraftMaid Cabinetry*

Right and opposite page:
Splashes of bright color were used in a Tuscan kitchen to add warmth. The ruddy color of the textured wall and the greenish hue of the windows are repeated in the hand-woven rug on the floor. The finely carved motif on the mantle hood is found in the island, and in the tile border above the countertops. This kitchen generates warmth, feels inviting and lived-in, and is a place where friends and family gather for large meals and lots of laughter. *Courtesy of Wood-Mode*

Sturdy legs on the island unit serve little function in way of structural support. They were put there to create the impression of the massive furnishings once crafted for homes of yesteryear.
Courtesy of KraftMaid Cabinetry

Antique furnishings add authenticity to the aged look of this kitchen's cabinetry. The stove and copper mantle hood are framed in brick, adding grand scale to the kitchen. *Courtesy of Harrison Design Associates*

The owner of this kitchen wanted its design to combine her love of nature, art, old things with character, and country living. Reflecting an English country style, the kitchen features a concealed hood in the display shelf above the range; faux finish moldings to match the bleached and waxed pine cabinets; custom tile, marble, and butcher block countertops; and a soapstone sink and countertop. *Courtesy of Design Solutions, Inc./Designer Joni Zimmerman*

An antiqued finish and intricate carving create the impression that this cabinetry was crafted in another century. A wrought-iron chandelier adds country character, while columned legs frame the sink unit.
Courtesy of KraftMaid Cabinetry

Large arched glass doors make this kitchen feel like a solarium. Exposed distressed wood beams and stone tile flooring give the impression that people have gathered here for meals for many years.
Courtesy of Harrison Design Associates

Flagstone flooring, Provencal colors, and molded cabinetry provide old world atmosphere to a country kitchen. *Courtesy of Wood-Mode/Designer John A. Buscarello*

Detailed moldings in the cabinetry pair with fine features such as basket storage and arched cutouts for a sense of history in this kitchen space. *Courtesy of KraftMaid Cabinetry*

Below and opposite page:
A French chateau kitchen features cheery blue countertops and lots of attractive nooks for decorative and storage purposes. A mix of cabinetry finishes and styles adds interest and diversity to the room. The mantle hood and matching ceiling trim bring it all together. *Courtesy of Wood-Mode*

A kitchen dominated by blue and yellow tiles stays open to a dining area and family room. The results are fabulous, creating a space that is warm, comfortable, and inviting, not to mention ideal for entertaining. A professional sized range sits atop two ovens styled like old-fashioned wood stoves. *Courtesy of Design Solutions, Inc./Designer Linda Watson* (Continued on following page)

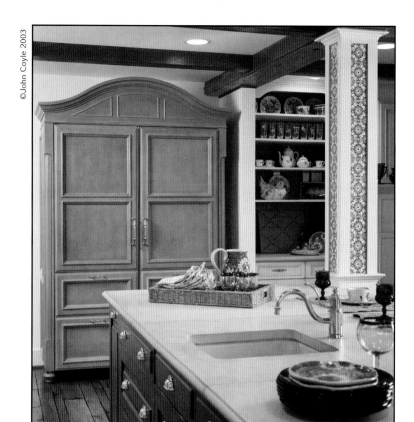

The crown molding that tops the cabinets is magnified in the base of the hood. A soft palette updates the look, rich in thick woodwork. *Courtesy of KraftMaid Cabinetry*

Set within the context of a great room, this kitchen area creates the effect of an outside wall using curtained display cabinets. An antique finish and detailed molding treatments on the cabinet faces is timeless. *Courtesy of Wellborn Cabinet, Inc.*

Exposed beams and warm colored cabinetry lend an aged air to this kitchen, where the kids can do homework at the island while Dad does the cooking. Distressed wood cabinets painted white provide contrast in the kitchen, and a wrought-iron chandelier sheds light over a multi-sectioned island for multi-tasking. The kitchen incorporates the family room, which maintains the old, French country flavor. *Courtesy of Design Solutions, Inc./ Designer Pam Kanewske*

The designers of this kitchen combined old world styling with cutting-edge contemporary to create a wonderful balance. *Courtesy of Miller/Dolezal Design Group*

Opposite page and following:
A mural was painted on the barrel-vaulted ceiling to bring the outdoors into the kitchen. Tiles breathe personality into the space, with the stove's colorful ceramic backsplash, the fruit and vegetable motifs, and the terra-cotta flooring. White custom cabinetry provides a welcome twist to old world elements. *Courtesy of Wood-Mode/Designer Barbara Ostrom*

©Philip H. Ennis

Photography by Willie Gibson

Hanging cook pots and an exposed plate rack are display tactics for creating a classic, European kitchen. Exposed brick adds the feeling of hearth to the space. *Courtesy of Crystal Cabinet Works/Designer Joyce Combs, Joyce Combs Kitchens, Ltd.*

A coffered ceiling sets the stage for a classic kitchen. Varying finishes on the cabinets include a natural wood finish strip under the crown molding, as well as a wood edge underscoring the granite countertops. The range hood provides a display area, making it the central focal point in a room luxuriously appointed in every detail. *Courtesy of Crystal Cabinet Works*

An arched cutout adds additional layers to the range area. Replacing the traditional hearth, this beautiful arrangement mimics the classic, replacing fireplace with six-burner stove and a double oven, flanked by two towers of handy pull-drawers. *Courtesy of Crystal Cabinet Works/Designer Kelly Wilson, Hayward Home Design Center*

A splendid reverse rotunda centers a room flanked with a fabulous curving stretch of windows. Ornamental carvings in the wood trim and corbels add classic flair to the cabinetry. *Courtesy of Crystal Cabinet Works/Designer Stan Ward, Dubuque Supply Company*

The dining area is separated from the rest of the kitchen in an adjacent room, but a large doorway allows the chef and his helpers plenty of contact with the dinner guests. Lamps flanking the kitchen sink add warmth and style to the space.
Courtesy of Harrison Design Associates

Black and white are softened with a mingling of tones – a marbled range hood, antique finish on the white cabinetry. By mixing finishes and styling unites to look like free-standing furnishings, this kitchen takes on a lived-in feel. *Courtesy of Crystal Cabinet Works/Designer Brad Fortune, Diversified Cabinet Distributors*

Two sinks make this kitchen extra efficient, and big windows make it bright. A wrought iron light fixture and carved panels on the cabinetry add years to the modern space. *Courtesy of Wood-Mode/Designer Franco Nonahal, Kitchen Studio*

Turned posts and a vintage finish on the cabinets
add to the kitchen's English country theme.
Courtesy of Wood-Mode

A recessed cook center is the focal point of this classic kitchen, where wall cabinetry is minimized. Instead, porcelain tile is used to evoke French marble inlays, from the floors and countertops to the backsplash. *Courtesy of Crossville Porcelain Stone/USA*

Period English antiques, rock-crystal chandeliers, and magnificent window treatments were added to give the space, once used primarily by domestics, an infusion of warmth and richness. Layered textures create a sumptuous space in which a family lives and eats.
Courtesy of Robin's Nest

An arched entryway and picture window create a European sensibility in this kitchen. Tile flooring, countertop, and backsplash are typical of southern European kitchens.
Courtesy of Crossville Porcelain Stone/USA

Entertaining was the main objective when designing this classic French provincial kitchen. The expansive center island is perhaps the kitchen's most exciting feature, creating a haven for culinary demonstrations and social gatherings. A light limestone backsplash was chosen to provide contrast to the darker cherry wood cabinets. Accent tiles with a grapevine pattern adorn the custom-made wood range hood. The floor features oversized African slate tiles for a rustic French touch. *Courtesy of Architextures Interior Design, LLC*

Photography by Klineberg, Inc.

Accessories like the wrought-iron chandelier, the blue and white delft-style pottery, and enameled ware add timeless charm. *Courtesy of Crystal Cabinet Works/Designer Brian Fagan, Distinctive Interiors*

A contemporary kitchen boasts elements reminiscent of the old world. Antique glazed cabinetry, mantle hood, and carved details in combination with modern appliances make the kitchen a place where the family can gather and where friends can feel right at home.
Courtesy of Design Galleria, Ltd.

Cut out arches and twisted columns add fanciful Italianate atmosphere to this bright kitchen. The curvaceous candelabra over the central island and eating counter is repeated in the dining nook beyond. *Courtesy of Crystal Cabinet Works*

A Swedish country kitchen is painted yellow to keep the sun in at all times, even on the dreariest of winter days. A mantle hood opens up to a blue and white tile backsplash with a border repeated above the counter on another wall. Countertops are Silestone®. Other features include the suspended spigot next to the stove and the extra sink of the small bar area. *Courtesy of Wood-Mode* (Continued on following pages)

In a nod to Bacchus, the grape and wine motif is repeated throughout this wonderful, spacious kitchen, in hand-carved wood details, a tile mural, and in the wine rack and wet bar that sit center stage under curved display cabinets. *Courtesy of Crystal Cabinet Works*

Camel glass in the island cabinets and a custom window invoke ancient cathedrals. The diamond and triangular shapes are repeated in tiling, and even the shadows cast by a metal basket hung on the range hood. Pull drawers replace the contemporary standard of shelving in the lower cabinetry areas of the kitchen, enhancing the feeling that this kitchen was shipped intact from a former home in the French countryside.
Courtesy of KraftMaid Cabinetry

An enormous leaded glass window seems to have been there for years, as do the exposed timber frames, textured mantle hood, and unfinished-stone floor. This kitchen serves up loads of cabinet, storage, and display space. A small dining area is tucked away, in a wood paneled nook. Overall, the space is grand yet comfortable. *Courtesy of Wood-Mode*
(Continued on following page)

The designer enhanced the integrity of this traditional style kitchen by creating an atmosphere that amplifies the joys of love, life, laughter...and cooking! Antique furnishings like the country French farm table and 19th century clock were selected to enhance the charm of the Provence style. Color was added with the window treatments, accessories, and carpet. The look of the cool and modern stainless steel appliances and fixtures was integrated through the addition of polished English brass cabinet pulls. *Courtesy of Elements in Design* (Continued on following pages)

Photography by John Canham

Photography by John Canham

Photography by John Canham

A talented artist painted a stone wall near the kitchen's ceiling to give the impression of age. Earthy colored tile flooring, the stove's blue tile backsplash, and tile walls with a hot air balloon motif add a touch of old world to this contemporary kitchen. *Courtesy of Wood-Mode/Designer Florence Perchuk*

In the true Tuscan style, large beams support the wood ceiling, stretching across the room at the fur down level to bring the height of the room to a more human scale. Artistic murals show through walls aged by faux finishes, giving the impression of walking through a quaint Italian village. Floor tiles imported from Italy are studded with cobalt blue glass inserts to maintain the color scheme established by the lower cabinets, murals, and the amazing stovetop backsplash. *Courtesy of Depew Design Interiors*

Splashes of bright color add warmth and interest to a kitchen dominated by earth tones. Stone framing the stove and fireplace, and the exposed distressed wood beams give a rustic appeal to the space. *Courtesy of Harrison Design Associates*

Finely-crafted cabinetry in a rich finish with carved moldings sets this kitchen's style. Slate-colored countertops complement the steel oven door, while the fridge wears cabinetry camo.
Courtesy of Yorktowne Cabinetry

Gorgeous new cabinets achieve the look of heirloom furniture through the use of decorative accents, like the crown molding build-ups, arched valances, and nickel grape valance appliqués. *Courtesy of Yorktowne Cabinetry*

Stonework over the range ties in with the nearby fireplace and makes a nice accent in a kitchen dominated by classic wood tones. *Courtesy of Wellborn Cabinet, Inc.*

A faux finish on the walls adds years and lots of character to a contemporary kitchen. An elegant chandelier provides even more personality, while colorful window treatments keep the atmosphere casual and comfortable. *Courtesy of Buena Vista Faux & Mural Painting*

Stainless steel appliances fit right into the old-time feel invoked by tile backsplashes and flooring. Earth tones emanate warmth, and a display shelf above the stove adds decor. *Courtesy of Crossville Porcelain Stone/USA*

BATHROOMS

This bathroom features dramatic craftsmanship with old world appointments. Individual elements are seamlessly executed, wrapped in colors of curry and azure. *Courtesy of Miller/Dolezal Design Group*

Photography by Patrick Wadley

Hand-carved ornaments have been applied to the faces of these cabinets, in a style popular for centuries. *Courtesy of KraftMaid Cabinetry*

French country styling adds up to luxury in this master bathroom. While soaking in the tub, one enjoys the view of a gorgeous window treatment and elegant light fixture that distinguish this sanctuary. *Courtesy of Design Express, Ltd.*

Photography by John Martinelli

A stucco dividing wall, a raised bath set in the shadows of Corinthian columns, fine cabinetry, and hand-painted tiles add the detailing of days gone by. *Courtesy of Crystal Cabinet Works/ Designer Stan Ward, Dubuque Supply Company*

The classic dry sink gets a glamorous update. Here it's no longer dry, of course, and wall cabinetry turns it into a complete vanity area. *Courtesy of Wellborn Cabinet, Inc.*

Fluted columns, crown molding, and a cap of creeping ivy add Italianate splendor to this lavatory setting. *Courtesy of Crystal Cabinet Works/Designer Brad Fortune, Diversified Cabinet Distributors*

Opposite page:
A fresh and elegant approach to design creates an inviting bathroom, where getting clean was never more satisfying. Sage colored tiles splashed across the bathroom, a decorative pillow, and a painting above the bathtub add color to the otherwise neutral-toned space. *Courtesy of Harrison Design Associates*

Photography by Real Images

Exposed beams climb the soaring roofline, setting the stage for a dramatic bathroom. Within these spacious boundaries, detailed cabinetry provides luxurious storage. Indigo-finished beadboard creates a contrasting blue backdrop. Basket storage adds hand-wrought flair. *Courtesy of KraftMaid Cabinetry*

West Indies and old world styling combine to create a bathroom rich in tradition and texture. Finely carved cabinet details, and the tile floor and tub are reminiscent of European ancestry, while exotic elements provide the tropical flavor. *Courtesy of Wood-Mode*

A wonderful finish on the enamel tub looks like the old steel tubs of long ago. Rich curtains and topiary appear right out of a castle, perfect in a timber-lined setting tucked under the eaves. *Courtesy of KraftMaid Cabinetry*

Bathroom cabinetry features heavy carvings, a bonnet pediment, French cabriole legs, and an antique distressed furniture finish to create a Cabernet master bath. *Courtesy of Wood-Mode*

What is a bathroom for if not to pamper and indulge oneself in luxury? A chandelier, draped fabric, and fabulous floral arrangements inspire the lady of the household to stay in the bathroom for hours. *Courtesy of Harrison Design Associates*

A bath tiled from floor to ceiling exudes a sense of soft elegance. Display shelves set into a rounded wall provide space to add decorative details or store toiletries. A distinctive vanity features a large bowl for a sink and a faucet mounted to the wall. The look is timeless and the feeling unforgettable. *Courtesy of Crossville Porcelain Stone/USA*

Venetian glass accent tiles shimmer like water on the walls. An aged patina added to the tiles adds history to the bath, while a sink mounted on a wrought iron stand adds character. *Courtesy of Crossville Porcelain Stone/USA*

An enormous shower stall tiled in refreshing aqua features an extensive bench and a clever alcove. A repeated motif in shimmery tiles adds movement and interest. *Courtesy of Crossville Porcelain Stone/USA*

Richly decorative tiles add old world ambiance to these baths, where time seems to slip away. Here, luxury gives way to comfort and warmth. *Courtesy of Crossville Porcelain Stone/USA*

CONTRIBUTORS

Aged Woods, Inc.
2331 East Market St.
York, PA 17402
800-233-9307/717-840-0330
www.agedwoods.com

Architextures Interior Design, LLC
7905 Big Bend Boulevard
Saint Louis, MO 63119
314-961-9500
www.architexturesllc.com

Buena Vista Faux & Mural Painting
P.O. Box 320553
Los Gatos, CA 95032
408-298-7531
bvartists.com

Crossville Porcelain Stone/USA
P.O. Box 1168
Crossville, TN 38557
931-484-2110
www.crossville-ceramics.com

Crystal Cabinet Works
1100 Crystal Drive
Princeton, MN 55371
800-347-5045
www.ccworks.com

Depew Design Interiors
248 Addie Roy Road, Suite B106
Austin, TX 78746
512-347-9876
www.depewdesign.com

Design Express, Ltd.
50 Skippack Pike
Broad Axe, PA 19002
215-641-1840

Design Galleria, Ltd.
351 Peachtree Hills Avenue NE
ADAC, Suite 234
Atlanta, GA 30305
404-261-0111
www.designgalleria.net

Design Solutions, Inc.
582B Bellerive Dr.
Annapolis, MD 21401
800-894-7349/410-757-6100
www.dsikitchens.com

Elements in Design
618 Island Place
Redwood Shores, CA 94065
650-595-8884
www.elementsindesign.com

Harrison Design Associates
3198 Cains Hill Place NW, Suite 200
Atlanta, GA 30305
404-365-7760
www.harrisondesignassociates.com

KraftMaid Cabinetry
15535 South State Avenue
Middlefield, Ohio 44062
800-571-1990/440-632-5333
www.kraftmaid.com

Miller / Dolezal Design Group
3000 Alpine Road
Portola Valley, CA 94028
650-529-2700
www.millerdolezal.com

Plain & Fancy Custom Cabinetry
Route 501 & Oak Street
Schaefferstown, PA 17088
800-447-9006
www.plainfancycabinetry.com

Robin's Nest
28 North Street
Hingham, MA 02043
781-740-4843

Wellborn Cabinet, Inc.
38669 Highway 77
Ashland, AL 36251
256-354-7022
www.wellborncabinet.com

Wood-Mode Fine Custom Cabinetry
One Second St.
Kreamer, PA 17833
877-635-7500
www.wood-mode.com

Yorktowne Cabinetry
100 Redco Ave.
Red Lion, PA 17356
800-777-0065/717-244-4011
www.yorktowneinc.com